The Artist's Suitcase

26 Essentials for the Creative Journey

Kent Sanders

SANDERS COMMUNICATIONS

The Artist's Suitcase: 26 Essentials for the Creative Journey

Copyright © 2015 by Kent Sanders, KentSanders.net

Published by Sanders Creative Media

All rights reserved. No portion of this book may be reproduced, stored in a retrieval system, or transmitted in any form or by any means—electronic, mechanical, photocopy, recording, scanning, or others—except for brief quotations in critical reviews or articles, without the prior written permission of the publisher and author.

While the author has made every effort to provide accurate URL's throughout the book, the author does not assume any responsibility for changes that occur to websites after publication of the book. The author does not have control, and does not assume responsibility, for third-part websites or their content.

Cover design by Kristi Griffith at Thumbprint Creative Arts, GoThumbprint.com.

Edited by Jim Woods, JimWoodsWrites.com.

Scripture quotations are from The Holy Bible, English Standard Version® (ESV®), copyright © 2001 by Crossway, a publishing ministry of Good News Publishers. Used by permission. All rights reserved.

*For my junior high English teacher,
Mrs. Mathis,
who encouraged me to write.*

Contents

Foreword   vii
Introduction   ix

A is for Attitude   1
B is for Blank Page   4
C is for Critics   7
D is for Doubt   11
E is for Excellence   14
F is for Failure   18
G is for Generous   21
H is for Humility   25
I is for Imperfections   28
J is for Just   31
K is for Key   34
L is for Love   37
M is for Mind   40
N is for Napkin   44
O is for Old Things   48
P is for Persistence   52
Q is for Quirky   56
R is for Redemption   59
S is for Secure   63
T is for Time   68
U is for Unfinished   73
V is for Variety   77
W is for We   80
X is for Xerox   85
Y is for Year   89

Z is for Zither   95
Epilogue: The Artist's Manifesto   99

Quick Favor   107
Gratitude   109
Who is Kent Sanders?   113
Notes   115

Foreword

Whenever I post anything on my website that Kent Sanders has written, reader engagement spikes—dramatically!

Why? Because Kent's writing strikes a chord deep within people's hearts about topics that matter to them. People immediately want to share their thoughts, ask their questions, and discuss the topics even further.

As I read through this book, I had a similar reaction. I wanted to pause and reflect on any number of thoughts that Kent shared. I wanted to camp out on one or two ideas from each chapter for days. So I did!

I encourage you to do the same. While Kent has written each chapter in a way that is clear and succinct, I hope you won't rush through this book. I hope you'll take ample time to absorb and consider how you can assimilate each of these ideas into your own life—perhaps using each chapter as a daily dose of inspiration for your soul.

On a personal note, I would like to say that Kent is not

only a great writer, speaker, facilitator, worship leader, and teacher, he's also a great friend. If you don't know him already, I'm glad to introduce him to you.

I hope you'll take Kent's words to heart as if they were written specifically for you, from one friend to another. As you read through this book, you'll find that it's true.

Eric Elder, Founder of TheRanch.org

Introduction

I know we've just met, but let me ask you a question. And I want you to be honest. *Really* honest. It's just you and me.

Do you ever feel like you've lost your way as a creative person?

If so, I can relate.

I remember the day vividly. It had been a long day of teaching, and it was almost time to head home. I wanted to enjoy a few minutes of silence before fighting traffic, so I slouched down in my office chair and stared at the bookcase next to me.

I was exhausted. I was in my mid-30's and 40 lbs. overweight. I thought about the courses I was teaching: Introduction to the Arts, Worship Leading, Speech, Technology for Worship, Guitar, and Introduction to Film.

All of these courses, in some way or another, were based on creative expression. The irony was that I felt anything but creative. The energy and enthusiasm of my

20's was long gone. I had no clear vision for my future, and I felt like a complete failure. I had lost my mojo and had no idea how to get it back. I knew I had to make some changes in my life to recapture the energy and momentum I once had.

Maybe you feel like I once did. Can you answer yes to any of the following?

- Do you feel like you've lost your way as an artist?
- Are you stuck in your creative life and in need of some inspiration?
- Do you need somebody to remind you that your creative work matters?
- Do you need to get your creative mojo back?
- Do you need permission to be yourself and follow your creative passion?
- Are you looking for practical advice on navigating doubt and fear, dealing with critics, figuring out your priorities, and taking control of your time?

If so, this book is for you!

The Artist's Suitcase is a call back to the basics. Just as the ABC's are the foundation of the English language, this book is a reminder of some of the basics for artists. Whether you write, paint, act, dance, sing, play an instrument, design graphics, or do some other type of creative work, this book is for you.

The Artist's Suitcase has twenty-six chapters, one for each letter of the alphabet. You might notice that the chapter titles don't all match—there's a mixture of nouns, adjectives, and even an adverb and a conjunction. In addition, don't take the "26 Essentials" in the subtitle too literally. These aren't necessarily "essential items" for the creative journey, but rather twenty-six chapters full of practical wisdom and inspiration for artists.

Just like in life, everything in this book isn't neat and perfect. I hope you'll embrace the joy and messiness of the artist's life. Wherever you are on the creative journey, it's always good to remember the essentials.

I also want you to know that I've written *The Artist's Suitcase* as a person of faith. This isn't a book of sermons, but I will occasionally use verses from the Bible or make other references to my faith. It's simply part of who I am. If you are a Christian, great! But if you don't share my faith perspective, that's okay, too. You'll still find a lot of content that will be helpful to you as an artist.

Before we set sail, let me make a few suggestions about getting the most out of this book:

1. Read it in a way that suits you. The chapters aren't sequential (except for the order of the alphabet), so jump around to whatever sections interest you. You can read the whole book in less than two hours. On the other hand, you can read a chapter a day and process the material in a deeper way.

2. Keep a notebook handy. I've included a few questions at the end of each chapter to help you apply the material. This is where the real learning takes place. Keep a notebook handy to write down your answers to the questions.

3. Read the book with a friend or group. Life isn't meant to be a solo adventure. The journey is so much better with friends! Ask a friend to read the book with you, or better yet, form your own reading group so you can learn together.

There's nothing in the world like being an artist. I'm so glad you picked up this book and am honored to be your traveling companion.

Oh, and one more thing: when you pack your suitcase, be sure to make room for a zither. (That will make sense in the last chapter.)

Thanks for taking the journey with me.

Kent Sanders

A is for Attitude

It's no coincidence that the word "attitude" begins with the first letter of the alphabet. A great attitude is the most important character quality you can possess. It's more important than talent, education, or titles. Your attitude is the most important factor that determines your level of success.

Some people are like thermometers. Their attitudes are a reflection of the conditions around them. When times are good, they are happy and cooperative. When times are bad, they are irritable and unproductive.

But successful people are like thermostats. They don't just react to the environment, they determine the environment. They have decided in advance to be positive and productive no matter what's happening around them.

John Maxwell, American's foremost expert on leadership, said, "Attitude is one of the most contagious qualities a human being possesses. People with good attitudes tend to make people around them feel more positive. Those with a terrible attitude tend to bring others down."[1]

How do you maintain a positive attitude when you don't feel like it? How can you start to function like a thermostat that changes your environment rather than a thermometer that just reflects it?

The answer is that having a great attitude is a matter of choice, not circumstances. Here are three strategies I have found helpful in staying positive. I call it the "3G" approach:

1. Grin. Sometimes you have to act the part before you start feeling it. If you are in a bad mood, start smiling anyway. Talk to people as if you're happy to see them. Act as if you have energy and enthusiasm. Pretty soon, you'll start to feel happier and more alive.

2. Gratitude. There's nothing like gratitude to help shake you from complacency or a bad mood. Take out a sheet of paper and write down five things you are thankful for. Pretty soon you'll realize how blessed you are. Even better, thank another person for something they have done for you.

3. Give. A bad attitude feeds on itself and makes you focus on your own problems. Start focusing on others and their needs. Giving to others is a great way to improve your attitude. Think of how you can help someone in a tangible way. Encourage someone with an email, text message, or even a shout-out on social media.

It's hard to be positive when there are so many discouraging things in life. But your attitude is a matter of choice.

When you choose a positive attitude, you'll inspire others and make yourself more valuable. A change on your inside will always show on the outside.

Questions for Reflection

1. Do you tend to be more like a thermometer or thermostat?
2. Who is someone in your life who has a positive attitude? How does their attitude affect those around them?
3. What are some challenges you face in developing a positive attitude?
4. How does a great attitude affect your ability to be creative and make great art?
5. What are five things you're thankful for?
6. What is a practical way you can give to another person today?

B is for Blank Page

The blank page represents the space where you create your art. It can be a computer, studio, canvas, or a literal blank page. When you look behind the page you'll see two creatures: the Monster and the Muse.

First there is the Monster. The Monster feeds on fear and likes to taunt you with these kinds of thoughts.

- *This won't be any good.*
- *Nobody likes what you're doing*
- *You'll never be a real artist.*
- *When are you going to give up these silly dreams?*

Every time you think about quitting, you feed the Monster. Every time you tell yourself your art doesn't matter, you feed the Monster. Every time you listen to the naysayers and doubters, you feed the Monster. Every time you let your dreams slip out the back door of your life, you feed the Monster.

Steven Pressfield calls this force "Resistance." In his landmark book *The War of Art*, he writes, "Resistance has no strength of its own. Every ounce of juice it possesses comes from us. We feed it with power by our fear of it."[1]

The Monster feeds on fear. You must starve it to death.

But there is also the Muse. The Muse is a magical creature that brings out the best in you. The Muse speaks words of life, hope, and beauty:

- *You were born for this*
- *You're making a difference in people's lives*
- *There are people who love what you're doing*
- *You have amazing potential*

The Muse feeds on faith and it is the wellspring of creativity within you. (As a person of faith, I believe God has an awful lot to do with this.) The Muse gives you the power to inspire, teach, and bless others.

Every time you pick up your pen or paintbrush, you feed the Muse. Every time you put your head down and do the work, you feed the Muse. Every time you improve your skills, you feed the Muse. Every time you serve someone with your art, you feed the Muse.

Look behind every blank page and you'll find the Monster and the Muse. One feeds on fear. The other feeds on faith.

Which one will you feed?

Questions for Reflection

1. How often do you battle the Monster? How often do you feel inspired by the Muse?
2. Which people in your life help feed your faith?
3. How are you helping another artist feed his or her faith?
4. When is the last time you thought about quitting? Where were you so frustrated?
5. When is the last time you pushed past the fear and kept going? What gave you the courage?

C is for Critics

The 2007 movie *Ratatouille* tells the story of Remy the rat, an unlikely chef at the renowned Gusteau's restaurant. The food critic Anton Ego pays a visit and shares some interesting insights about criticism in his review:

> *In many ways, the work of a critic is easy. We risk very little, yet enjoy a position over those who offer up their work and their selves to our judgment. We thrive on negative criticism, which is fun to write and to read. But the bitter truth we critics must face, is that in the grand scheme of things, the average piece of junk is probably more meaningful than our criticism designating it so.*[1]

Critics have their place and you can often learn something from them. Even criticism offered in the wrong way can be helpful if you approach it the right way.

So how exactly do you learn from your critics? When someone criticizes you, there are five key questions you should ask to maximize your growth and learning.

1. What is the source? All criticism is not created equal. If your critic is a negative person you may just be the latest in a string of verbal assaults. But if the critic is a friend, sit up and take notice. Proverbs 27:6 says, "Faithful are the wounds of a friend; profuse are the kisses of an enemy." A true friend is someone who cares enough to point out a flaw you need to correct.

2. What is the issue? Have you heard this criticism before? Is there a pattern of behavior you need to address? I'm a college teacher, and at the end of every semester I ask my students to evaluate each course. I want to know what I can improve the next time I teach a course. If several students say the same thing, I know I should pay attention.

3. Is there a kernel of truth? Sometimes there is truth in what a critic says. If it's delivered in a loving way, it's much easier to accept. But if someone criticizes you in a hurtful way, it's difficult to admit there might be some truth to it.

4. What can you learn? Criticism can be a stumbling block or a stepping stone. It all depends on how you use it. It's a stumbling block when you don't learn from it and discover whether there's any truth to the criticism.

It's a stepping stone when you swallow your pride and learn something. The lessons may not be pleasant, but it can make you a better artist or leader.

One of my favorite quotes comes from Teddy Roosevelt:

> It is not the critic who counts; not the man who points out how the strong man stumbles, or where the doer of deeds could have done them better. The credit belongs to the man who is actually in the arena, whose face is marred by dust and sweat and blood; who strives valiantly; who errs, who comes short again and again, because there is no effort without error and shortcoming; but who does actually strive to do the deeds; who knows great enthusiasms, the great devotions; who spends himself in a worthy cause; who at the best knows in the end the triumph of high achievement, and who at the worst, if he fails, at least fails while daring greatly, so that his place shall never be with those cold and timid souls who neither know victory nor defeat.[2]

Learn from your critics and let them help you become a better artist. But realize that in the end, it takes a lot more guts to create art than to criticize it.

Questions for Reflection

1. When was the last time someone criticized you? Was there any truth to the criticism? What did you learn from it?

2. Why do artists tend to take criticism so personally?
3. Do you think the work of a critic is easy, as Anton Ego said in Ratatouille? Why or why not?
4. How can you become better at giving constructive criticism to others?

D is for Doubt

When I started to write this book, I went to the local library, opened my computer, and stared at the screen for a while. Then I wrote this:

> *I'm afraid to write something. I'm afraid to commit something to paper (or screen) because it won't be good. I'm afraid to take this leap forward, writing this book, just knowing that it won't really help anyone. The problem is, I don't know how to start this. Honestly, I just want to play Angry Birds for a while and shut my brain off.*

The root of doubt is fear. When you're afraid, you begin to doubt yourself, your talent, and your creative calling. We usually think of doubt as the absence of belief, but that's not true. Doubt is believing in advance that you're going to fail. The fear of failure is powerful and can keep you from reaching your creative potential.

At one time or another each of us has wrestled with these three fears:

1. "I'm afraid my work isn't good enough." Sometimes you're afraid to move forward because you're waiting for perfection. You see others who are doing great work and enjoying success, and you don't think you measure up.

Perfection is a terrible taskmaster because you'll never reach it. Instead, pursue excellence in your art and learn to improve as you go. Each of us has to start somewhere.

2. "I'm afraid of what others will think." Sometimes you don't take action because you're waiting on someone to give you permission. You're looking for a thumbs up, a pat on the back, or a sign that it's OK to move forward.

Be careful that your need for affirmation doesn't grow into a codependent need for someone's approval. Even well-meaning people can give you advice that can derail your calling if you let it. If you can't make a decision without having to consult a specific person, you might have unhealthy need for their approval. Don't let someone hold your dreams hostage.

3. "I'm afraid I'm going to fail." Sometimes you're paralyzed by fear because you're waiting for a guarantee. You want assurance that others will accept you and that your dreams will become reality.

But this guarantee doesn't exist. It's possible that you'll fail, that others will ignore you, that your dreams won't come true.

That's OK because failure is an important part of the creative journey. There will be times when you strike out. But there will also be times when you knock it out of the park.

Henry Ford said, "If you think you can do it, or you think you can't do it, you are right."[1]

Don't let doubt rule your life. Believe in yourself, believe in your gifts, and believe in the One who has called you to this wonderful, crazy journey we call the artist's life.

Questions for Reflection

1. What doubts do you have about yourself, your gifts, or your creative calling?
2. Is there anyone whose approval you tend to seek? Why do you think their approval is so important to you?
3. How would you go about your work if there were a guarantee you would succeed? What is stopping you from doing that now?
4. Are you waiting for a gatekeeper to give you permission to pursue your art? If so, what can you do to move forward anyway?

E is for Excellence

There is a lot of misunderstanding these days about what excellence means. We can easily confuse excellence with perfectionism.

Some artists will sacrifice almost everything on the altar of perfectionism. They will ignore their family, health, and any sense of balance so they can be the best. This drive to be more successful than everyone else comes from a deep insecurity within the artist.

Here's how I define excellence: *Excellence means doing the right things in the right way for the right reasons.*

Let's look at three practical ways to pursue excellence:

1. Do the right things. This is all about your priorities. If you are completely obsessed with your work but ignore your health, family, finances, or spiritual growth, you are not practicing excellence. You're not just an artist. You're a real person with a multi-faceted life, and your art is only one aspect of it.

My first job after graduating from college was leading worship at a church in northern Illinois. I was newly married and excited about the future. The people in the church were great, I was a good fit for the position, and I loved my job. In fact, I loved it a little too much.

During the first few years of my marriage, I worked an unhealthy amount of hours and wanted everything in my ministry to be the best it could be. I didn't have a sense of boundaries and I pursued "excellence" to the neglect of more important things (namely, my wife).

My sense of self-worth was so closely tied to my ministry "success" that I couldn't separate the two. It was an unhealthy and dangerous way to live. Fortunately, I learned from my mistakes. After being married for almost twenty years, today I have much better boundaries and a healthier view of excellence.

2. Do things in the right way. This is all about your attitude. It means taking the time and effort to do your best work with the resources available to you. You may feel you don't have enough time, money, personnel, or training. That's OK because your most important resource is your attitude.

The Disney Imagineers are some of the most creative people on the planet. In their book *The Imagineering Way*, they write, "Every new project at Imagineering starts with the assumption that it will be fun and exciting. We never say we don't really want to do it this way—we do it the best way we know how. We are our end users because we like the product."[1]

Do you approach your work with the same amount of enthusiasm?

3. Do things for the right reasons. This is all about your motives. Why do you create in the first place? You do it for enjoyment, but it goes deeper than that. The ultimate purpose of creative expression is to glorify God and serve others with your gifts.

It's tough to keep a healthy sense of excellence. T help me stay balanced, I have a picture of my wife and son as the wallpaper on my iPhone. Every time I look at my phone I'm reminded why I need to be excellent. It also reminds me that there's more to life than being an artist.

When you pursue true excellence, you will know when to work hard, but you'll also know when to stop.

Questions for Reflection

1. Do you agree with my definition of excellence? Why or why not?
2. Have you ever let your priorities get out of whack? Why did this happen, and what were the results? What are you doing now to help keep your priorities in order?
3. Be honest with yourself and think about your motives. What is driving you to be an excellent artist? Is it healthy? Unhealthy?
4. What visual reminders do you have (i.e. a photo

or object) that help you keep a healthy sense of excellence?

F is for Failure

One time a student sent me an email that said, "The take-home exam has the answer key on the back of it. Did you mean to do that?"

Oops. Professor fail.

We all make mistakes. Sometimes it's messing up a take-home exam, and other times it's more serious.

Once I advised a music student who had taken a part-time youth ministry. He served in the position for two years even though he didn't enjoy it. He was angry with himself and felt like he had wasted two years of his life. I told him that I didn't see it as a failure; it was actually a blessing to have so much clarity on what you shouldn't be doing.

It's hard to look at failure and see it as something positive. But with the right perspective, a failure can become a stepping-stone to success by following these four steps:

1. Don't beat yourself up. It's easy to feel bad about yourself when you mess up, but it doesn't help you move toward your goals. It only drives you further into negative thoughts and actions. When you fail, respond with thinking and reason rather than just emotion.

2. Figure out what went wrong. Why did you fail? What thoughts or feelings led to the failure? Were there any habits that contributed to the problem? See if you can pinpoint what happened.

3. Develop a plan for success. What do you need to do now? What's your strategy? Have you ever heard the saying, "If you fail to plan, you're planning to fail?" A plan will help you stay on track and give you a better chance of avoiding the mistakes that led to the failure in the first place.

4. Link arms with others. You will be much more successful with the help of others than you are by yourself. Are you involved in a small group or support team of some kind?

C. S. Lewis said, "Failures, repeated failures, are finger posts on the road to achievement. One fails forward toward success."[1]

Failing at something doesn't mean you're a failure. You can make mistakes, you can fail, you can take a two-year detour, but you're only a failure when you stop learning. So keep reaching, keep growing, keep pressing on. If you approach your failures correctly, you will find that they are stepping-stones to greater things.

Questions for Reflection

1. Have you ever felt like you wasted a year or two (or more) of your life pursuing something that didn't pan out? What did you learn from it?
2. Why is it so hard to see failure in a positive light?
3. What was the last failure you experienced? How did you deal with it?
4. Who is on your support team? What can you do to develop or strengthen those relationships?
5. Think of a person you personally know who has bounced back from failure. What did you learn from their example?

G is for Generous

It's human nature to put yourself first. This isn't anything new. The book of Genesis tells the story of Cain and Abel, who both made an offering to God. When Cain saw that God accepted Abel's offering but not his own, he killed Abel out of jealousy. He was looking out for himself.

As children, we learn that there is a better way to live. We hear it in phrases like "'Tis better to give than receive," or "Sharing is caring." We learn that there's more to life than looking after yourself.

A few years ago I interviewed author Jeff Goins on the topic of generosity, and he made a simple but profound statement: "Being generous is its own reward. When you give, you get."

On my journey as a writer, I have been amazed at the generosity of people who have nothing to gain from being generous. It would seem like successful people don't have time to help others who have a smaller platform than they do, but it's not true. The most successful people know the value of being generous.

Why? Because they understand the difference between a scarcity mentality and an abundance mentality.

A person with a scarcity mentality believes there is not enough to go around. They are jealous of other's success, money, accomplishments, or possessions. They believe that life is like a giant see-saw where other people's success results in their failure.

A person with an abundance mentality believes that there is plenty to go around. They know that when others succeed, it can help them also. They also know that when they are generous to others, it comes back to them in unexpected ways.

Being generous doesn't mean you give everything away for free. Generosity is not about economics. It's about orientation. A generous person is oriented toward serving, helping, and giving to others.

Here are ten easy ways to be generous:

1. Buy a good book for a friend.
2. Donate your time or talent to a ministry or organization that needs your help.
3. Send a handwritten thank-you note to someone who has helped you.
4. Thank someone on social media so others can see it.

5. Leave a thoughtful comment on someone's blog.
6. Help promote other people's art on your blog, newsletter, or social media.
7. Make an introduction between two friends who could help each other.
8. Open doors for people.
9. When a retail employee is helpful, ask to speak to their manager and tell them how helpful the employee was to you. (You can also do this when you're talking to a customer service rep on the phone. It blows them away because it's so unusual.)
10. Post a comment on a friend's Facebook wall telling a friend you are praying for them. (You can also send a text message.)

There are many other ways. You get the idea.

A generous person is like a powerful river where the water is constantly flowing. It gives and receives, nourishing the land all around it.

A selfish person is like a stagnant pond that keeps all the water to itself. It always receives but is never able to give.

When in doubt, always be generous. You will be happier, more successful, have better relationships, and be a much bigger blessing to the world.

Questions for Reflection

1. Why is it so hard to be generous?
2. Have you seen generosity be its own reward in your life? How?
3. Do you tend to have a scarcity mentality or an abundance mentality? What is the difference between the two?
4. How has someone been generous to you? How did you thank them?
5. Look through the list of ten ways to be generous. Which one could you put into practice today?

H is for Humility

In July 2011, Adam Bevell experienced something he'll never forget.

He had traveled from his home in Arizona to see U2 in Nashville during their 360 tour. Many U2 fans travel a long way to see their favorite band, but Bevell is no ordinary fan. He is a blind guitarist, and he had come to Nashville in hopes of getting on stage to play with his hero Bono.

Bevell came prepared with a sign that read, "BLIND GUITAR PLAYER. BRING ME UP." He held it up all through the concert as he stood in the crowded pit near the stage.

The last song U2 played on the 360 tour was "Moment of Surrender." As they finished the song and began to walk offstage, Bono noticed the sign and asked Bevell what he wanted to play. He responded, "All I Want Is You" (he and his wife's favorite U2 song) and Bono had him escorted onstage. A stagehand gave him Bono's guitar and Bevell began strumming.

Bono began to sing and the rest of band joined in for the spontaneous performance. When the song was done, Bono hugged Bevell and even gave him his guitar![1]

At the end of a long and exhausting music set, in front of 45,000 adoring fans, one of the world's most famous musicians shared the spotlight with a blind guitar player.

Whether you have 45,000 fans or just four or five, it's a challenge to share the spotlight and stay humble. Here are several truths to help keep you grounded:

1. Your talent is on loan from God. You are a steward of the talent God has given you. It's not really yours in the first place. You can't claim any credit for the good things that happen as a result of your talent. All the glory goes to God.

2. Your true friends love you for you who are, not what you do. Those who matter most in your life don't love you because of your talent or gifts. They love you unconditionally as a friend or family member.

3. Your self-worth shouldn't come from your success. It's easy to be so emotionally tied to your art that you feel like a winner when things are going well, and a failure when things aren't. Don't base your self-worth on temporary success or failure.

These three truths can help you keep a healthy perspective on your creative gifts. They will also put you in the right frame of mind to relate to others.

Saint Augustine pointed out the true path to greatness

when he said, "Do you wish to rise? Begin by descending. You plan a tower that will pierce the clouds? Lay first the foundation of humility."[2]

If you had been in Josh Wilson's shoes that night, what would you have done? Would you have stepped away from the microphone to help someone else?

Questions for Reflection

1. How can you maintain a healthy sense of confidence, yet also remain humble?
2. Think about your fans versus your friends. Friends love at all times, but fans are much more fickle. Which group do you spend more time thinking about and serving?
3. Do you see yourself as a steward of your creative gifts, or as an owner? What's the difference?
4. Have you ever done something out of rivalry with another artist? How can you avoid doing the same thing in the future?

I is for Imperfections

I love to visit the St. Louis Art Museum. Whenever I go, I always set aside time to study Van Gogh's paintings. There's something special about seeing them up close and in person. It's different than looking at them in a book. I get as close as I can without stepping over the guard line and being accosted by security.

The view is completely different up close. You notice the lumps of paint on the canvas. Straight lines become crooked. Perfect shapes become a little unbalanced. Bold strokes become blobs of paint.

What looks so flawless at a distance is full of imperfections when you get up close. This is the difference between art made by machines and art made by humans.

Take music, for example. Machines make music that is perfect but has no soul. People make music that is imperfect and sprinkled with flaws, but human.

The Beatles made an astonishing amount of great

music, but most of it isn't perfect. It's filled with mistakes, imperfections, and oddities here and there. Yet no one would argue that it diminished the greatness of their music. (For a complete list, visit the site What Goes On: The Beatles Anomalies List.)[1]

In an age of computerized perfection, it's easy to feel pressure to produce flawless art. But we don't consider a work of art "great" because it's perfect. We think of "great art" as something that's full of passion and humanity, something that represents hard work, creativity, and achievement. An original Van Gogh is priceless, but a printed poster of the same painting only costs a few dollars.

When it comes to your art, are you a "glass half-empty" or a "glass half-full" kind of person? The answer explains how you think about your imperfections.

A "glass half-empty" artist only sees what's missing. He only focuses on all the things he could have done better.

But a "glass half-full" artist sees the beauty, goodness, and truth he has added to the world. It may not be perfect, but he's created something wonderful that wasn't there before.

It's easy to look at the glass of your creativity and see what you didn't achieve. But at the end of the day, even if the glass is half full, you have still filled it with something worthwhile. A person dying of thirst would be just as grateful for a glass half full as they would a full glass.

And we do live in a thirsty world—a world thirsty for grace, empathy, and truth. You can offer all of that and more through your art and your life.

You don't need to have a huge platform. You don't need a publishing deal. You don't need a showcase in an art gallery. You don't need a recording contract.

All those things are great, but they are not necessary. The only thing required is a willingness to do the work and put your art out there for people to experience.

Whatever you have to offer, even if it's imperfect, is a welcome gift to world thirsty for beauty and truth.

Questions for Reflection

1. Do you struggle with being a perfectionist? What do you think is driving this need to be perfect?
2. What's something you've created that wasn't perfect? Did the flaws detract from someone's enjoyment of it?
3. Have you ever noticed mistakes in music or a movie? Did the mistakes make you enjoy the movie less?
4. Why are we sometimes so gracious toward others but so hard on ourselves?

J is for Just

Every artist wonders if their work really matters in the vast scheme of things. With a few billion people in the world, can one person's creative contribution make any difference?

Yes! I know it's a cliché, but art can change the world. Of course, not all art changes the world, and a lot of art changes it for the worse. But art has the potential to make a positive difference.

You should never say, "It's just art."

Are you just an architect? Ask Isidore and Anthemius when they laid down the blueprint of the great Hagia Sophia and said, "We think we can do this."

Are you just a painter? Ask Michelangelo after he put the finishing touches on the Sistine Chapel.

Are you just a writer? Ask J. R. R. Tolkien after he wrote a little book that began, "In a hole in the ground there lived a hobbit."

Are you just a musician? Ask the Beatles after they appeared on the Ed Sullivan show in 1964.

Are you just an actor? Ask Meryl Streep after receiving 19 Academy Awards nominations (and 3 wins).

Are you just a dancer? Ask Michael Jackson after he performed the Moonwalk on Motown's 25th anniversary special in 1983.

Are you just a filmmaker? Ask George Lucas about May 1977 when he flew to Hawaii during the premiere of his new space movie because he was sure it was going to flop. It was a little film he called *Star Wars*.

It's never "just art." In God's economy, there are no "justs." He gave you a specific set of creative gifts to use at this time and place in history. You're one of a kind! If you don't do what you do, it won't get done.

So don't think of yourself as "just an artist." You're so much more.

You're a dreamer.

A doer.

A thinker.

A creator.

A visionary.

A leader.

A risk-taker.

An unlocker of potential.

And a thousand other things.

But one thing you will never be is a "just." And you will never make "only art."

If you ever hear someone say, "It's just art," they are

correct in one sense—it just has the power to change a life. It just has the potential to inspire a child who will one day do some extraordinary. It can just make grown men cry, give hope to the hopeless, and change a person's entire perspective.

F. Scott Fitzgerald wrote, "Having once found the intensity of art, nothing else that can happen in life can ever again seem as important as the creative process."[1]

Every movie, every song, every poem, every innovation, every feat of engineering, every courageous voyage, and every leap forward for humanity was the result of the creative process.

It's only art, and it only has the power to change the course of history.

Questions for Reflection

1. Have you ever thought of yourself as "just an artist"?
2. Have you ever heard someone diminish the importance of the arts? How did that make you feel? How did you respond?
3. Do you believe you have the power to change people's lives with your art? Why or why not?
4. How do you keep a balance between having big dreams and being realistic?

K is for Key

Did you know you have a very special key? It's not a key you'll find in a purse or a pocket, and it won't open a door or start your car's ignition.

You have a key that unlocks the creative potential of others.

Think of someone who has made a difference in your life. It might be a teacher, friend, pastor, or coach. He or she changed your life with their love, encouragement, and correction. They made an unmistakable impression on you that helped unlock your potential.

There are many people who have made a difference in my life. One of the most important was my junior high English teacher, Mrs. Mathis. She saw that I had the potential to be a writer and said, "I want you to dedicate your first book to me." This isn't my first book, but I've dedicated this one to her because she inspired me so much I remember it almost thirty years later.

You can do the same thing for others by helping unlock their potential. Here are two powerful ways you can have a positive affect on others:

1. Give them opportunities. One of the best parts of my job as a college professor is the chance to work with students. I love seeing students face challenges, often struggling at first, but then building confidence and finally succeeding.

There are people all around you waiting for a chance to prove themselves. They just need an opportunity. At one time or another, we have all depended on someone to give us a shot. You can pay it forward by doing the same for someone else. You could invite someone to sit in on a recording session, write a guest post for your blog, or finish a small task that could lead to something bigger.

Steven Spielberg said, "The delicate balance of mentoring someone is not creating them in your own image, but giving them the opportunity to create themselves."[1] You can help others unlock their potential by giving them opportunities to grow as artists.

2. Give them encouragement. The ancient philosopher Philo said, "Be kind, for everyone you meet is fighting a hard battle."[2] Don't underestimate the powerful effect your encouraging words can have on others.

One day in my mid-20's I was on a train heading back to Illinois, where I lived at the time. The train stopped at a small town, and a young man whom I'd never met before handed me a note right before he stepped off.

He must have overheard a phone conversation I had

about some discouraging things I was going through. Here is what the note said:

> *Do not be discouraged. Keep running the race that God has set for you. Do the work that God has planned for your life and trust Him to take care of the rest. Don't get down when things aren't running smoothly. Just trust God to take of them. Keep your chin up. :)*

Fifteen years later, I still have that note. I look at it now and then to remind me of the power of encouragement.

We all have a key that we use through our words and our actions. It's a key that can bring hope and healing, or inflict pain and suffering. How will you use your key? Whose potential can you help unlock?

Questions for Reflection

1. Think back on your life. Who helped unlock your potential as an artist? What did he or she specifically do to help you?
2. Look around at the people in your life. Who can you encourage? Who needs an opportunity?
3. Have you ever thought about encouraging a complete stranger, as the young man on the train did for me? What's stopping you?

L is for Love

Citizen Kane is universally recognized as one of the greatest films of all time. Orson Welles and his collaborators created a masterpiece that was well ahead of its time in storytelling, cinematography, and special effects. Yet for all its achievements, it's one of the saddest movies ever made.

The film tells the story of Charles Foster Kane, a wealthy businessman who began his career with good intentions. But, over time, he tries to control everyone around him. In the end he dies alone with a mansion full of treasures but a heart full of bitterness and regret.

Kane's onetime friend Jed Leeland summarizes the theme of the movie: "That's all he ever wanted out of life, was love. That's the tragedy of Charles Foster Kane. You see, he just didn't have any to give."[1]

Let me ask you a simple but profound question. Do you love the people you serve?

Love means doing what's best for others. The best way you can love others through your creative work is to make the best art possible. Love isn't a feeling. It's an action you demonstrate by serving others with your art.

Serving others out of love isn't a burden. It's a joy. It's the most fulfilling thing imaginable because you're not only sharing your art. You're also sharing God's love. We are God's vessels, and he will work through our creative gifts if we let him.

Henri Nouwen put it this way: "We are not the healers, we are not the reconcilers, we are not the givers of life. We are sinful, broken, vulnerable people who need as much care as anyone we care for. The mystery of ministry is that we have been chosen to make our own limited and very conditional love the gateway for the unlimited and unconditional love of God."[2]

When you use your God-given creative gifts, it's more than art. It's a ministry. You don't have to work at a church to be a minister. In fact, the word "ministry" just means "service." We're serving others with our art in the name of Jesus.

Love means that we stop seeing people as customers or clients. We see them as people to love and serve.

How do we show our love by serving others?

We serve by being compassionate.

We serve by being excellent.

We serve by being persistent.

We serve by being disciplined.

We serve by being humble.

We serve by being faithful.

We serve by being generous.

These qualities are action-oriented. The best way you can love others as an artist of faith is not just to talk about it, but to do it. When your art comes from a place of love, you not only serve God well. You also serve the people he loves.

We must avoid the tragic example of Charles Foster Kane, who couldn't receive love because he didn't have any to give. When we serve out of the depths of God's love, there's more than enough to go around.

Questions for Reflection

1. Have you ever thought about making great art as a way to show your love for others? Do you feel you have love to give through your art?
2. How are you currently serving others with your art?
3. Do you think of your art as a ministry? Why or why not?
4. Is it hard to see your clients and customers as people to love and serve? What would change if you began to look at them that way?

M is for Mind

Ask the average person to describe an artist, and you'll probably hear some of these words: emotional, sensitive, gifted, quirky, high-strung, non-conformist, genius, and many others. But "thinker" is not usually one of them.

We all think, of course. But we tend to associate the creative process with our emotions and feelings rather than our minds. The truth is that your mind is the source of all your creativity. Therefore, it's vital that you take good care of your mind by feeding it regularly.

So what kind of content should you put into your mind? These are the six most important types:

1. Books. Choose books that will help you grow and become a better artist and leader. It's important to read books from a variety of perspectives and subjects. This will keep you fresh and prevent you from getting into a mental rut. You should include great fiction books because you need to be inspired by great stories.

2. Podcasts. Podcasts are free and don't necessarily require extra time. You can listen to them while you're driving, exercising, or doing other activities. As a creative person, don't limit yourself to content focused on business or productivity.

3. Movies. Movies blend storytelling, moving images, and music to transport us into other worlds. Movies can also change your perspective and give you experiences you can't get any other way. Movies can speak to your heart and mind while sharpening your creativity.

4. Classes. Classes are a great way to get specialized knowledge and stay relevant in your field. Over the last year I have taken courses on writing for large websites, self-publishing, online teaching, and business. Some of these were free but required that I invest my own money.

5. Blogs. I subscribe to a few dozen newsletters and use unroll.me to "roll them up" into one daily email digest. That way, I can skim through the content without having dozens of emails clog my inbox.

The kind of content you put into your mind will determine your thoughts. Make sure you're reading, watching, and listening to great content every day.

I love this powerful quote from James Allen's classic book *As a Man Thinketh*:

> *All that a man achieves and all that he fails to achieve is the direct result of his own thoughts. . . . A man's weak-*

ness and strength, purity and impurity, are his own, and not another man's; they are brought about by himself, and not by another; and they can only be altered by himself, never by another. His condition is also his own, and not another man's. His suffering and his happiness are evolved from within. As he thinks, so he is; as he continues to think, so he remains.[1]

Who do you want to be, and where do you want to go? The answer will determine what to put in your mind. Earl Nightingale said it best in his classic work, *The Strangest Secret*: "We become what we think about."[2]

So what are *you* thinking about?

Questions for Reflection

1. Which of the six types of content listed above do you enjoy the most? Which do you enjoy the least?
2. Do you have a plan for reading and listening to great content? What would happen if you scheduled just 15 minutes a day for reading?
3. If you don't have enough time to read or consume good content, what activities could you cut from your schedule? Could you stay up a little later or get up a little earlier?
4. How does it feel to realize that your success is

the result of your thoughts? Does this make you happy or sad?

N is for Napkin

Consider the humble napkin. It's a simple dining accessory we take for granted. We use it to wipe our mouths and clean up spills, yet don't give it a moment's thought.

However, the napkin might be the most overlooked creative tool in the artist's arsenal. How many people have written great ideas on restaurant napkins when paper wasn't available?

For artists, the napkin is all about making use of what you have in the moment. When a great idea strikes or the right opportunity comes along, artists don't wait for circumstances to be perfect. They use whatever is available and get to work.

If you don't think you have enough resources, you're not alone. Everybody knows there will never be enough time or money to do everything you want.

But you can't let that keep you from starting. You have

to begin with what you have and build from there. Don't let your lack of resources become an excuse for not pursuing your dreams.

John Wooden, the famed UCLA basketball coach, describes the challenges he faced in building a championship team:

> *When I came out to UCLA from Indiana State Teacher's College in 1948, I had been led to believe we'd soon have an adequate place to practice and play our games. However, that did not occur for almost seventeen years. During that time, I conducted UCLA basketball practice in a crowded, poorly lit, and badly ventilated gym on the third floor of the Men's Gymnasium building. Much of the time there was wrestling practice at one end, a trampoline on the side with athletes bouncing up and down, and gymnastics practice on the other side. The gym was known as the "B.O. Barn" because of the odor when it was busy.*
>
> *... For sixteen years, I helped our managers sweep and mop the floor every day before practice because of the dust stirred up from the other activities. These were hardship conditions, not only for the basketball team, but for the wrestling and gymnastics team members and coaches as well. You could have written a long list of excuses why UCLA shouldn't have been able to develop a good basketball team there.*
>
> *Nevertheless, the B.O. Barn was where we built teams that won national championships in 1964 and*

1965. You must take what is available and make the very most of it.[1]

It's tempting to focus on the reasons you can't make great art. Instead, focus on what you do have and build from there.

The great hymn writer Fanny Crosby didn't let her limitations stop her. Although an incompetent doctor blinded her as a young child, she fell in love with poetry and wrote her first stanzas at age eight.

Fanny was also a zealous learner and could quote large sections of the Bible by heart, including the Pentateuch, the Gospels, and Proverbs. Crosby wrote over 9,000 hymns in her lifetime and personally knew many Presidents.[2]

It might feel like you don't have enough resources. It might feel like you have problems that are insurmountable. It might even feel like the whole world is working against you at times!

Don't let excuses hold you back. Take a look around. If you want to build something great, you have exactly what you need to get started.

Even if it's just a napkin.

Questions for Reflection

1. Do you feel you don't have the right resources to do the creative work you need? Why or why not?

2. Make a list of three things you think you need. (It could be time, money, connections, training, or something else.) Which is one is most important? What can you do in the next seven days to get more of that resource?
3. If you discovered you had one year to live, how would that change your sense of urgency and your perception of the lack of resources?

O is for Old Things

When it comes to art, do "old things" intimidate you? Do the classic works of painting, writing, sculpture, music, or even movies scare you a bit?

If so, you're not alone. Most people are intimidated by towering creative giants such as Shakespeare, Michelangelo, and Beethoven.

Let me put your fears to rest. You can understand and enjoy the great works of art and history. When you encounter them for yourself, you'll be inspired to do your own best work.

In his introduction to the spiritual classic *On the Incarnation* by Athanasius, C. S. Lewis speaks about the importance of experiencing the "old books" for yourself:

> *There is a strange idea abroad that in every subject the ancient books should be read only by the professionals, and that the amateur should content himself with the*

modern books. Thus I have found as a tutor in English Literature that if the average student wants to find out something about Platonism, the very last thing he thinks of doing is to take a translation of Plato off the library shelf and read the Symposium. . . . The error is rather an amiable one, for it springs from humility. The student is half afraid to meet one of the great philosophers face to face. He feels himself inadequate and thinks he will not understand him. But if he only knew, the great man, just because of his greatness, is much more intelligible than his modern commentator. . . . It has always therefore been one of my main endeavors as a teacher to persuade the young that firsthand knowledge is not only more worth acquiring than secondhand knowledge, but is usually much easier and more delightful to acquire.[1]

Lewis' words apply not only to books, but to all types of creative art. When we think of a work as one of the "greats," we tend to build it up in our minds as a towering accomplishment that only geniuses can understand. But most of the time, those works are great not because they're complicated, but because they're simple.

It's not enough to read about great art second-hand. You should experience it for yourself as much as possible.

But where do you start? It's easy to get overwhelmed by the sheer amount of great art available. So just pick one thing and dive in.

If you like painting, visit a museum in your area.

If you like music, listen to a recording of Beethoven,

Mozart, or modern greats like Miles Davis or the Beatles. Be sure to listen to the whole thing in one sitting to get the full experience.

If you like architecture, visit a local cathedral or historic site.

If you like to read, pick up one of Shakespeare's plays or Homer's *Iliad* or *Odyssey*.

If you like movies, watch one of the classics such as Charlie Chaplin's *City Lights* or David Lean's *Lawrence of Arabia*.

If you want to grow in your creative life, you have to stay curious. You must always be seeking out new things to learn and new artists to explore.

One of the best biographies I've read is Walter Isaacson's *Steve Jobs*. The book mentions several times that Jobs was a huge fan of Bob Dylan.[2] I didn't know much of Dylan's music, so I decided to educate myself.

I listened to several of his albums on Spotify, including *Blood on the Tracks*, *Bob Dylan*, and *Modern Times*. I was amazed at the power and simplicity of his music and wondered why I hadn't been listening to this my whole life!

When you read, watch, or listen to something new, it can often lead you to something else you'll enjoy. Every piece of art is like a map that leads to more treasures.

So take a little time to visit an art museum, pull a classic work of literature off the shelf, or sample a bit of older music. You'll find that ironically, the things of old will inspire you in ways that are fresh and new.

Questions for Reflection

1. Why do we tend to assume that the "classics" are harder to understand than contemporary works?
2. Is there a classic book you've started but didn't finish? Why not? What's stopping you?
3. Have you ever visited an art museum? What was your impression? (If you haven't, how could you arrange a trip in the next month?)
4. What do you think makes a work of art "classic"?
5. Do you think we have a bias toward newer art in modern culture? Why or why not?

P is for Persistence

One of Aesop's best-known fables is *The Tortoise and the Hare*. The hare challenges the tortoise to a race, confident he will win by a long shot. The race begins and the hare gets so far ahead of the tortoise that he takes a nap. When the hare wakes up, he finds that the tortoise kept moving and won the race.

You and I are a lot like the tortoise. It may take a while to get where we're going, but if we persist we'll eventually get there.

There are times when you'll feel like giving up on your creative goals. Maybe you're writing a book, building something, or making music. It's important to be persistent and work through the problems that make it harder to reach the finish line.

Here are five common reasons we want to give up, and how to deal with each of them:

1. Fatigue. Your physical fatigue affects your mind

and emotions. When you're physically depleted you don't have the willpower and the correct frame of mind to persevere through challenges.

Solution: Take care of your body and make sure you're getting enough rest. (The average adult needs eight hours per night.) Many people also find that a nap each day helps refresh them. I take a short nap almost every day.

In addition, cut down your intake of junk food and fast food. If you need to lose a few pounds, get on an exercise program. You only have one body, so treat it well.

2. Discouragement. Sometimes your problems seem to compound on each other and you just want to quit. It's much easier to run away from your problems than deal with them head-on. It's more tempting to veg out in front of the television or bury your frustrations in a week of binge eating than to do the hard work required for success.

Solution: Deal with your negative emotions in a healthy way. Go for a walk, write in your journal, or find other positive solutions to your problems. Running away will only make them worse.

3. Confusion. Have you ever lost your focus and didn't know which way to go? If so, you're not alone. Most people know what it feels like to become paralyzed by the stress of life and lose their direction.

Solution: Reconnect with your purpose and vision. Where do you want to be in one, two, or five years? Think about your long-term goals and the steps it will take to get there.

Ralph Waldo Emerson said, "What lies behind you and

what lies in front of you, pales in comparison to what lies inside of you."[1] When you get clarity on what lies inside of you—your purpose and vision—the way forward becomes clear.

4. Overwhelm. There are times when you've committed to too many responsibilities and you feel completely overwhelmed.

Solution: Prioritize your responsibilities. You can't do everything. For nearly a year, I hosted a weekly podcast. Despite the massive amount of work I had put into it, I decided to end it because it wasn't helping me reach my goals. Decide which things are the most important and focus on those.

Don't be afraid to say "no" to someone who requests your time. If you don't control your time, someone else will.

5. Regret. If you are beating yourself up over mistakes you've made, you won't be able to focus on the future. Regret can suck the life out of you and keep you from making forward progress.

Solution: Don't dwell on the past because you can't change it. Learn from your mistakes and apply those lessons to the present and the future. Focus on the one thing you can change, which is yourself.

Matthew Weiner, the creator of *Mad Men*, knows a think or two about persistence. He said,

> It took seven years from the time I wrote Mad Men until it finally got on the screen. I lived every day with that

script as if it were going to happen tomorrow. That's the faith you have to have.

Hollywood is tough, but I do believe that if you are truly talented, get your material out there, can put up with rejection, and don't set a time limit for yourself, someone will notice you.[2]

It's easy to get sidelined by problems on the creative journey. But you must persist and keep on doing the work you're called to do. There's too much at stake for you to throw in the towel.

Questions for Reflection

1. Which of the five areas listed above is your biggest frustration right now?
2. How much sleep do you get each night? Is it enough?
3. Do you feel clear about your direction in life? Why or why not?
4. Are you able to say "no" to others when their requests don't line up with your priorities? Are you OK with disappointing them?
5. Do you tend to dwell on the mistakes of the past? What have you learned from those mistakes?

Q is for Quirky

Artists have a reputation for being a little different. In some cases, it is even a point of pride. After all, who wants to be just like everyone else? It's okay to be a little quirky, right?

Well, yes and no. All of us have funny little habits and ways of talking or thinking that make up who we are.

Quirks are the peculiar little habits and oddities that make you who you are. Some examples of quirks:

- The co-worker who wears the same type of shirt every day.
- The girl who has a purple stripe in her hair.
- The kid down the street who is obsessed with Minecraft.
- The friend who only drinks his coffee black.
- The cousin who likes to wear mismatched socks.

- The guy who is obsessed with U2 and has seen them in concert seventeen times.

But here's the thing about quirks: You should never let your "quirkiness" become an excuse for not doing your best work. The key lies in the difference between quirks and character flaws.

Quirks are okay when they are part of your personality. Quirks can even help you be more creative. (I even have a few—okay, more than a few—myself.) But quirks cannot replace character.

Have you ever known someone who had character flaws, but just explained them away as being "quirky"? This is reinforced in culture by the concept of the "artistic temperament," which says artists are prone to being egocentric, moody, always late, and hard to work with.

Those are not quirks. Those are character flaws. Those are signs of immaturity and laziness. Those are the marks of an artist who may be an adult, but who's acting like a child. Those are the qualities of an artist who is not ready to be a leader and operate in the real world of deadlines, limitations, and teamwork.

A few months after I graduated from college, I landed my first full-time job as a worship leader at a church in northern Illinois. The official workday began at 9:00 a.m., but I usually didn't arrive until at least 9:15 or 9:30. I reasoned that because I was at the church several evenings a week, I should be able to come in a little later. I didn't see a problem with bending the rules as long as I got my work done.

Then one day, the senior pastor called me into his office and reprimanded me for always coming in late. (I really had no excuse since I lived next door.) I didn't like being corrected, but that incident made me realize that I wasn't exempt from the standards everyone else had to follow. My "quirk" of coming to work late was in fact hurting my reputation and productivity.

It's fine to be quirky, but you should never excuse bad behavior in the name of being a "quirky artist." Be authentic, and never pretend to be someone you're not. But be the best version of yourself—one who rises to the challenge, takes responsibility, and does such great work that others want to work with you.

Questions for Reflection

1. What do you consider to be your quirks? Do they help or hinder you in your creative work?
2. What quirks have others noticed in you?
3. Think about other creative people you've known. What were some of their quirks, and how did those characteristics affect their relationships or creative output?
4. Do you think you have an artistic temperament? Why or why not?

R is for Redemption

What do *The Wizard of Oz*, *The Shawshank Redemption*, and *Raiders of the Lost Ark* all have in common?

Answer: They're all movies with a message of redemption.

We normally talk about "redemption" in a religious context but the word has meaning far beyond that. Redemption is all about recovering something that's lost, delivering people from the clutches of evil, or setting the world right. It's making things the way they're supposed to be.

The Wizard of Oz tells the story of Dorothy, a farm girl who feels unappreciated and wants to escape from her boring life. A tornado sweeps her away to a grand adventure, and in the end she learns that there's no place like home.

In *The Shawshank Redemption*, Andy Dufresne is sent

to prison after being convicted of murdering his wife and her lover. He takes his friend Red's advice to "get busy living, or get busy dying," becomes influential in the prison, and eventually finds freedom on his own terms.

Raiders of the Lost Ark follows archaeologist Indiana Jones on a globetrotting adventure in search of the Ark of the Covenant. In a delicious thematic reversal of the Holocaust, God uses a Jewish religious artifact to defeat the evil Nazis.

These are stories of redemption where hope prevails, good triumphs evil, and the world is made right again.

Artists are agents of hope. With every note on an instrument, brushstroke on the canvas, or word on the page, you are weaving a story of redemption and helping set the world right.

As a guitarist, I've devoted a good chunk of my professional life to playing and listening to music. One of my favorite songs is Geoff Moore's "When All is Said and Done." The song reminds me of my priorities, and how my life won't be measured by my accomplishments and accolades. In many ways it's the theme song of my life.

There are countless songs that have inspired change and action. Here are a few:

- Steven Curtis Chapman's song "When Loves Takes You In" has inspired many families to consider adoption.
- For several decades, U2's "Where the Streets

Have No Name" has been an anthem of hope for equality and justice.
- The 1985 song "We Are the World" was a worldwide sensation that raised funds for humanitarian aid in Africa.

Redemption can shine through any kind of art. But how do you create redemptive art that brings hope to a dark world? There are two keys:

1. Redemptive art must be excellent. Whatever type of art you do, make every effort to do your best. No one pays attention to art that isn't done well.

2. Redemptive art must be authentic. People have to understand the darkness before they can appreciate the light. Don't hide your mistakes or your scars. Those are what make hope so compelling.

How does your art tell a story of redemption? How does it help set the world right? Is it a story of hope? Grace? Renewal? Forgiveness? Mercy? Reconciliation?

Your art doesn't need to change the whole world to make an impact. It just needs to change one person's world.

Questions for Reflection

1. Why is redemption such a universal theme in art?
2. What is a song, movie, poem, or other work of

art that has inspired you? How does it contain a message of redemption?

3. Do you think of yourself as an agent of hope? Why or why not? How does that change your perspective on your creative work?

4. Does it scare you a bit to be authentic in your art? Why are we sometimes so afraid to tell the not-so-pretty parts of our story?

S is for Secure

A few years ago our family decided to get a dog. We discovered a sweet Australian shepherd named Madison at the local animal shelter. She had been abused by her former owner and was terrified of men. It took several months before she would even let me pet her.

Madison has changed a lot over the last three years but she still needs constant affirmation. We could pet her for hours every day and it would still not fill her emotional tank. There's a part of Madison that will always be needy and insecure.

The word insecure means "subject to fears, doubts, etc.; not self-confident or assured."[1] You and I can easily fall into this emotional state if we're not careful. As artists, we crave approval and affirmation. But we can take it too far if we are not emotionally healthy ourselves. As an artist who is constantly putting your work out there, you must be secure in your identity and self-worth.

If you want to be a more secure artist, it helps to recognize the signs of insecurity. This is useful for identifying and correcting our unhealthy emotional patterns. It's easy to see these patterns in others, yet completely miss them when it comes to our own hearts.

By the way, how do I know these five signs so well? Because I have been guilty of all of them at times. Maybe you have as well.

1. An insecure artist constantly finds fault with others. When my son Ben was in fourth grade, I had a conversation with him about school bullies. He asked why some kids pick on others. I explained that some people feel so badly about themselves that the only way they can feel better is to drag everyone else down with them. Sadly, some people keep doing this way past the fourth grade.

2. An insecure artist can't accept constructive criticism. No one likes to be criticized, but even the most stinging criticism can contain a kernel of truth. An insecure person is not mature enough to see the kernel of truth and learn from it. They can dish it out, but can't take it.

Early in my teaching career I received a nasty email from a student. He criticized me pretty harshly about my leadership of our music program. I felt angry that he had the nerve to send me such a critical note. Plus, I wanted to dismiss his comments since he wasn't a good student.

But in my heart I knew the truth: there was a bit of accuracy to his statements. There were several areas in which I was coming up short.

3. An insecure artist always wonders what everybody else thinks. He can't make his own decisions because he is too concerned about other people's approval. He is constantly asking what everyone else thinks about this or that.

When others give you advice, treat it like a set of crutches. They can help you move in the right direction, but rely on them too long and you'll eventually be too weak to stand on your own.

4. An insecure artist relies on external measurements for his sense of self-worth. There are many ways that insecure people measure their worth: their car, house, clothing, personal appearance, titles, friends and associates, income, size of their business or organization, degrees and awards, and even the success of their children.

None of these things is bad. In fact, they can all be wonderful things when put in the proper perspective. But none of them is a true measurement of your value as a person. I have known a lot of people with money, academic degrees, and all kinds of outward signs of "success," yet who were unhappy and insecure.

You can't base your self-worth on the shifting tides of people's opinions and other external measurements. Instead, base your confidence on these three things:

- Knowing who you are (confidence in your gifts and purpose).

- Knowing who loves you (confidence in the unconditional love of those closest to you).
- Knowing whose child you are (confidence in your eternal standing as a beloved child of God).

5. An insecure artist sees everyone as a competitor. He doesn't have the emotional maturity to compliment, encourage, or publicly support others without expecting something in return. He can't be happy for other people when they succeed; he thinks a win for someone else means a loss for him.

I mentioned this idea in the chapter on generosity, but it's so important it bears repeating: An insecure person sees success as a limited pie where there's only so much to go around. If you get a bigger piece, that means there's less for me, right?

A secure person sees himself and everyone else as having unlimited potential for success. He doesn't see others as competitors, but as fellow travelers and on the creative journey. He knows that your success means his success, and vice-versa. He knows that a rising tide lifts all ships.

Secure people create art from a place of generosity.

Insecure people create art from a place of fear.

Guess which type of person has more fun? More friends? More influence and success?

Walt Disney said, "Somehow I can't believe there are many heights that can't be scaled by a man who knows the secret of making dreams come true. This special secret, it seems to me, can be summarized in four C's. They are Curiosity, Confidence, Courage, and Constancy, and the greatest of these is Confidence. When you believe a thing, believe it all over, implicitly and unquestioningly."[2]

If you want to reach your creative potential, you have to belief in yourself, link arms with others, and serve with a generous heart. Creativity is an inside job.

Questions for Reflection

1. As you look at this list, do any of these qualities describe you? Which ones?
2. Where do you think a sense of insecurity comes from?
3. Do you feel confident in your gifts and purpose?
4. Do you tend to see others as competitors or as collaborators?
5. Do you struggle with accepting constructive criticism from others? Why or why not?

T is for Time

Question: What is the most precious resource you own?

Maybe you thought of a car, a house, a piece of jewelry, or a bank account. When we think of valuable items, we immediately think of material things.

But time is actually the most precious thing you own. It's the one thing you can't get back. You can always get more money or another car. But that's not true with time. Once it's gone, it's gone forever. No one knows how much they will have, so it's important to use it wisely.

So how do you use time well? Here are three key strategies:

1. Learn to say "no." When people ask you for a commitment, sometimes it's easier to say "yes" because you don't want to hurt their feelings. But remember that every time you say "yes" to another commitment, no matter how small, you have to say "no" to something else you're already doing. You can't keep putting more things on your plate without taking something off.

If you don't have enough time for your creative work, you must prune your schedule. Take a hard look at your current commitments and evaluate whether you should continue them.

Sometimes it can be costly to say "no." One of the worst decisions I've ever made was starting a network marketing business selling memberships to a nutrition company. After a few weeks, it was obvious that I was not a good fit for this business. I knew it was going to fail. Even though it had cost over $2,000 to start the business, I decided to cut my losses and move on.

If you want to stay focused on your priorities, you will pay a price. Sometimes you will pay the price of passing up an opportunity. Sometimes you will pay the price of upsetting someone. Sometimes you will pay a financial price, as in my case. But that's the price of staying focused on your art and pursuing success.

2. Take advantage of spare moments. Spare moments are small chunks of time between other events. Five minutes here, or ten or fifteen minutes there, can be very useful if you use them intentionally.

Here are some examples of spare moments:

- Waiting at your doctor's office.
- Waiting at the DMV (Dept. of Motor Vehicles) to renew your license.
- Waiting to pick up your child from school.

- Waiting for a class or meeting to start.
- Waiting for someone to arrive at lunch.
- Waiting for your spouse to finish shopping.
- Waiting in line at the grocery store.

Notice how all of these moments involve waiting. It's inevitable that you will spend time waiting for something to start, or waiting for other people. You can't always avoid waiting, but you can determine how you will use your time. Will you spend your waiting time passively or purposefully?

These spare moments are a gold mine for being productive or doing creative work. Here are a few ways to take advantage of them:

- Read a good book. You should always have a book with you. This is the beauty of eBooks; you have a whole library at your fingertips.
- Think about topics or other content ideas for blog posts or podcasts.
- Respond to emails, calls, or messages.
- Send up a few quick prayers.

If you don't take control of your schedule, someone else will. Be intentional about using your time, especially the spare moments that we tend to waste.

3. Use your drive time for personal growth. According to the U.S. Census Bureau, the average commute time for Americans is 25.4 minutes.[1] That's almost five hours of time in the car each week. My own commute is 30 minutes each way.

The best way to make use of your car time is to listen to podcasts or audiobooks that will help you become a better artist, leader, spouse, or parent. You can get the equivalent of a part-time college or grad school education without leaving your car.

Most people get into their cars, crank up the radio and shut off their brains. But you can take advantage of this time to grow in your skills.

To be honest, I don't listen to audio training every moment I'm in the car. I will often listen to a podcast on the way to work, and then listen to music on the way home. I don't have a set routine. But on a typical week I listen to several hours' worth of personal growth material. (I also use my exercise time to listen to podcasts.)

It's easy to feel overwhelmed by your commitments. But it's up to you to take control of your schedule. When you say "no" strategically, use spare moments, and take advantage of your drive time, you will get a much better return on your investment of time.

Questions for Reflection

1. Do you have a hard time saying "no" to others? Why or why not?
2. What is a current commitment that you would like to say no to? What is the risk of

getting out of this commitment? What is the reward?
3. What is a recent time when you were waiting somewhere? How did you make use of that time? How could you have used it better?
4. Do you have a daily commute, and if so, how long is it? What are some things you could do during your commute to help you stay productive?

U is for Unfinished

All around the world, in homes, offices, and studios, there are unfinished works of art that will never see the light of day. Does one of them belong to you?

When I'm sitting in my college office, I see lots of great art. On the wall to my right are movie posters for two of my favorite films, *Citizen Kane* and *The Searchers*. On the wall to the left there is a print of Rembrandt's masterpiece *The Return of the Prodigal Son*.

On the bookshelf beside me are models for some of my favorite vehicles, including the Millennium Falcon from *Star Wars*, the DeLorean from *Back to the Future*, and the Mach 5 from *Speed Racer*.

The bookshelves behind me hold hundreds of books and DVD's. The iPhone on my desk contains hundreds of songs, dozens of podcast episodes, and a few dozen apps.

And the MacBook I'm using to write this book on is a work of art in itself too.

All these items were created by people who finished their work. These products and works of art began as ideas in someone's mind, but they didn't stay that way. Their creators worked on the concepts (usually collaborating with others) and the ideas began to take shape. But most important, they finished their work.

This is where it's easy to get sidetracked. You have a great idea, you start to work on it, and you build momentum. You might even share it with a few people. But then as you work on it, you start to lose steam. Life gets busy, you lose focus, and you don't finish your work.

Sometimes our work ends up like the movie *Superman Lives*. You say you've never heard of this movie? That's because it was never made.

In the 1990's, Warner Bros. decided to resurrect the Superman franchise. They cycled through a few directors before landing on Tim Burton, who had given the studio great success with his Batman movies.

Screenwriters worked on several drafts of a script. Production staff worked on sets and special effects. Nicholas Cage was cast as the Superman and filmed screen tests with the redesigned costume.

But after years of development and endless problems, the studio shut down production. A great deal of time and energy, not to mention millions of dollars, went down the drain and *Superman Lives* was never finished. What could have been one of the most interesting movies from the 1990's ended up as just another "might have been."

Everyone has a "might have been" story. It may not be a

big Hollywood movie, but I'll bet you've started something you'd love to finish. It might be a book, a piece of music, a painting, or something you're building or making with your hands. You want to finish it, but you just can't seem to find the time.

In the bottom of someone's desk drawer, there is an Oscar-winning screenplay. It just needs to be finished.

On someone's hard drive, there is a life-changing novel. It just needs to be finished.

In someone's closet, there is a painting worthy of display in a gallery. It just needs to be finished.

On someone's college transcript, there is a degree listed with most of the required classes already taken. The degree could open doors and unlock someone's potential. It just needs to be finished.

In someone's journal, tucked away on a bookshelf, are sketches that could be the basis for a comic strip or an animated movie. They just need to be finished.

On someone's sketchpad are drawings for a remodeled kitchen, basement, or treehouse. They just need to be finished.

On someone's CD's or hard drive are rough demos of Grammy-winning songs. They just need to be finished.

Is that someone you?

If so, what can you do to turn your "might have beens" into reality?

What creative art do you still have unfinished?

Questions for Reflection

1. Why is it so easy to start creative projects, but so hard to finish them?
2. Have you worked on something (a book, painting, poem, blog, song) that you haven't yet finished? What's keeping you from finishing it?
3. Think of your life six months from now. What would it feel like to have that project finished? What could it do for your business and self-confidence?
4. What are some of the hurdles you face in finishing your projects, and how can you take action in spite of them?

V is for Variety

One day I was working on a big project with several college students. We were getting hungry and I offered to run through Taco Bell and grab lunch. As I left, one of the students said, "Make sure to get a lot of Fire sauce packets!"

I had eaten at Taco Bell many times before but never used their condiments. This time I decided to give it a shot, just for kicks. When I sat down to eat, I emptied a packet of Fire sauce onto my taco and took a bite.

It had a great flavor and a little kick. I loved it!

From that moment, I was hooked. Now when I eat at Taco Bell, no item feels complete without The Fire. I even keep a few packets in my college office in case of a culinary emergency.

We all tend to get stuck in routines that don't allow for change, growth, or new ideas. And that, my friend, is a place you don't want to be. It's a town called Complacency, and it's just down the road from Boringville and Stagnant City.

Sometimes you need a little push to shake things up and get out of that creative rut. Here are twenty ideas for trying something new and adding a little variety to your life.

- Watch a movie or TV show you haven't seen.
- Read a different type of book than normal (i.e. fiction, non-fiction, graphic novel). Check out the Amazon bestseller list for ideas.
- Read a screenplay. (Check out The Script Lab website for lots of free screenplays.)
- Read an author you completely disagree with to gain a new perspective.
- Go to the library and browse through a different section than usual.
- Follow someone on Twitter who posts interesting updates.
- Subscribe to a new blog.
- Visit a historical site in your city.
- Get a cool photography app on your phone and take some fun pics.
- Visit an Art museum.
- Listen to a new podcast.
- Get out of bed earlier.
- Listen to some new music.
- Find the closest kid younger than ten and build or draw something with them.

- Buy a toy for yourself.
- Visit a bookstore.
- See if you can spot Jupiter, Saturn, or (if you're got an eagle eye) Mercury using the StarWalk app or the SkyAndTelescope website. If you use good binoculars or a small telescope you can see Saturn's rings and Jupiter's Galilean moons.
- Send a handwritten note instead of an email.
- Learn to draw, paint, or do movie editing.
- Learn to play an instrument (or a new one).

Variety is the spice of life. Try something new and shake things up. Who knows, you might even learn something from a tiny packet of sauce in a fast-food restaurant.

Questions for Reflection

1. Why is it so easy to get into a creative rut? Are you in a creative rut now?
2. What is the last new thing you tried? Did you like it?
3. Have you done any of the items in the above list in the last six months? What was the result?
4. Is there a friend or family member who might be in a creative rut? How could you help them experience something new?

W is for We

The Fall of 2011 was an exciting time to live in St. Louis. The Cardinals were performing poorly in the regular season, then unexpectedly roared back to win the National League playoffs. In the World Series against the Texas Rangers, the Cardinals pulled off a dramatic last-minute win in Game 6 and went on to win the series.

A handful of players—Albert Pujols, Chris Carpenter, David Freese—received the lion's share of attention (and deservedly so), but the dramatic win would not have been possible without the whole team.

This is a good illustration of how artists should operate. You're not a one-man or one-woman show. Even if you mainly work alone, you still need others to accomplish your work.

It's rare that an artist can do something extraordinary on his own. There is almost always a team behind the scenes. We see this principle at work in the movie business.

There may only be a few names on the movie poster, but when the credits roll you see that it can take hundreds, sometimes thousands, of people to make a film.

If you want to rise to your full potential, you have to join with others in community. Here are six places to find communities for networking and support to help you be a great artist.

1. Church. Churches should be the most creative places around. However, many artists don't have an opportunity to use their gifts at church. Some churches don't make much of an attempt to reach out to artists, or are limited in their view of the creative arts.

That being said, I have made it a point to be involved in churches where I've been given opportunities to use my creative gifts. I've also made many great lifelong friends through creative arts ministries, worship teams, and small groups.

If your church could use some help in its outreach to artists, speak to your church leaders. This might be a sign that you are the person to help your church in this area!

2. Masterminds. A mastermind is a group of people who meet on a regular basis to help one another with their business goals. The concept of a mastermind has been around a long time, but it was popularized by Napoleon Hill in his book *Think and Grow Rich*. (It's a tremendous book if you haven't read it. It's unfortunately titled because it's not really about getting rich.)

My mastermind meets on Monday morning via Skype. There are currently three members, and we have a strict one-hour format. We begin with each person taking a few minutes to share any progress we've made toward our goals. We spend the rest of the time with one person in the "hot seat" sharing about a specific problem or issue in their business. The rest of us ask questions and offer feedback.

Being a part of this mastermind has been extremely helpful because I know the others in the group are going to ask about my goals. It gives me motivation to keep working toward them. I've also gotten ideas and feedback that has been immeasurably helpful.

To find our more about mastermind groups and how you can join or create one, check out Pat Flynn's webinar on building a mastermind group. You can also visit my the Resources page on my website for many more tools and resources related to personal develop, leadership, and creativity.

3. Facebook Groups. Facebook groups are a great way to connect with like-minded people. I am involved in several active groups on a range of topics: self-publishing, writing, business, ministry, and productivity. I've met lots of wonderful people and have gotten loads of great ideas that have helped my life and business.

4. Networking Sites. There is a networking site for every conceivable interest. The one that has been most valuable to me is Dan Miller's 48DaysEagles.com. The home page explains the purpose of the site:

You know you were born to be an entrepreneur. You've felt the nudge to "do your own thing" for a while now (maybe even your whole life), but where do you start and how do you conquer the fear and overwhelm of starting your own business? Dan Miller's 48 Days Eagles Community helps driven, smart, creative individuals like you who are willing to take action to break free from monotony, find your true purpose, and create not only work, but a full life you thrive in.

I have met dozens of great friends through 48days.net. It has been the single biggest catalyst for growth as a writer and creative entrepreneur.

5. Local Artist Groups. Online networking can be helpful, but don't discount the value of face-to-face interaction. Depending on your interests and type of creative work, you can find local groups that provide feedback and opportunities for networking. Don't overlook art shows, festivals, and special events in your area.

6. Other Bloggers. I have made many valuable connections with other writers and artists through their blogs. The secret to developing a good relationship with other bloggers is to give before you expect something in return. Subscribe to their newsletter, make insightful comments on blog posts, and share their posts on social media. Be genuinely interested in what they're doing and don't just view them as someone who can help you.

When you put the focus on helping others, you will gain credibility and influence because people know you're the real deal. Then they will be more likely to help you in return.

The creative journey is much more fun with others, so take the initiative to get involved with people whom you can serve, and who can help you in return. You can accomplish so much more with a "we" than a "me."

Questions for Reflection

1. Are you more of an introvert who likes to be alone, or an extrovert who enjoys being with others? How does this affect your view of the need for community in your life?
2. Which of the above groups do you currently participate in? How has it impacted your life?
3. Which of the above groups would you like to get involved in? What can you do in the next seven days to make that happen?

X is for Xerox

"Xerox" is a term we don't hear much anymore. It originally referred to the company that pioneered the photocopier, but over time it came to refer to almost any kind of copying process. Once in a while you will still hear someone use the phrase "make a Xerox" or "Xerox that document."

That's okay for making copies, but not so good for making artists.

As a kid growing up in the 1980's, I idolized Michael Jackson. I loved the red zippered jacket he wore in the "Thriller" video and was jealous of the kids at school who had one. Sometimes I would try to channel the magic by putting a white marching band glove on my right hand and doing the Moonwalk. (I promise not to subject you to the horror of watching me dance.)

The problem was that I wasn't Michael Jackson. I

didn't have his talent. I could try as hard as I wanted, but I could never be him.

The world doesn't need another Michael Jackson. Or Leonardo da Vinci or Miles Davis. Or Picasso, Steven Spielberg, Harper Lee, Steve Jobs, or anyone else who has made great art.

What the world needs is the one and only you.

One of my favorite podcasts is *The Accidental Creative* by Todd Henry. I love the phrase he uses at the end of each episode: *Cover bands don't change the world.*

So how do you keep from becoming an artist who's like a cover band that plays everyone else's hits, but has none of their own? How do you stay true to yourself and your gifts, yet still learn from others? How do you stay authentic in a world that values conformity?

There are many possible answers to those questions, but I'll highlight four proven practices. Look into the lives of all the great artists, and you'll see these common threads.

1. Follow your passion. When you're doing work that excites you, that's when you're the most authentic. Do you look forward to your work, or do you feel it's sucking the life out of you?

Two helpful ways to begin following your passion are learning about your personality and discovering your strengths. There are plenty of tests available, but here are free versions of two popular ones: the DiSC personality profile, and a strengths assessment.

2. Be true to yourself. Don't be a people-pleaser. Staying true to yourself means that you'll disappoint people sometimes. That's okay. Your job is not to make everyone else happy, but rather to follow your God-given creative calling. It may take some time to get there, but you must stay on the path that makes the best use of your passion and gifts.

3. Take the road less travelled. It's hard to take a risk when you see others falling in line and conforming to others' expectations at the expense of their calling. But don't be afraid to be your own person. Whatever you do in life, you will make mistakes. So you might as well be doing something you love.

4. Hang around with dreamers. The more you associate with successful people who believe in making dreams a reality, the more you will think like them. That's why it's so important to get involved with people who are positive and forward thinking.

So let me ask you: Who is influencing your thinking these days?

When I was a kid my Dad would sometimes tell this goofy joke: "How do you catch a unique rabbit? Easy. Unique up on him."

You, my friend, are unique. There's no one quite like you. Never has been, never will be. If you don't do the creative work that only you can do, you're robbing the world of your unique gift. And that would be a tragedy.

Oscar Wilde said, "Be yourself; everyone else is already taken."[1] Don't let your life become a Xerox of someone else's dreams.

Questions for Reflection

1. Do others have expectations for your future? If so, what are they? Are these expectations valid?
2. Why is it so hard to travel your own path in life and possibly disappoint others?
3. How would you describe your passion in life in 1-2 sentences?
4. Think about the people you spend the most time with. Are they positive and forward thinking, or pessimistic and stuck in the past?

Y is for Year

Here's a little exercise to get your creative juices flowing.

Take out a sheet of paper and draw a line down the middle. At the top of the left-hand column, write today's date. Take a few moments to think about your life. Write down several areas you want to improve. It might be making more money, paying off debt, losing weight, getting a different job, taking a special trip, writing a book, or finishing an important creative project. This part of the exercise shouldn't take too long because you know the areas of your life you want to change.

Now at the top of the right-hand column, write the date one year from now.

Close your eyes and clear your mind. Take a few deep breaths and block out everything around you. Don't think about what you have to do today or all the distractions happening around you.

Imagine what your life could be like one year from today. How could it be different? Would you have more energy or a better income? What about that book, blog, music, or other project you're working on? What would it feel like to have it finished?

In the right-hand column, underneath the date a year from now, write down what you see—your appearance, energy level, success, and the other items that are important to you. This is what your life could be like one year from now.

A year is both a short time and a long time. It can seem short because it does go by so quickly. But a year is also plenty of time to accomplish something great if you use your time well. We tend to overestimate what we can accomplish in a day and underestimate what we can accomplish in a year.

Let's do a little math. What if you spent just one hour each weekday working on a major goal or project? Over the course of a year, that adds up to over 250 hours, or over six 40-hour workweeks.

What could you do with the equivalent of an extra six weeks over the next year? You could write a book, start a book, open a business, get healthier, learn a new creative skill, start a podcast, plan an overseas trip, write a musical, or any of a hundred other things.

So how do you use a year to its full advantage? These five practical strategies have helped me the most:

1. Set goals that will stretch you, but are

Y is for Year

realistic. When I think about my annual goals, I try to aim for 25% more than what I think is realistic. This way, the goal is still in the realistic range, but it will stretch me beyond what I think is possible. (For a great book on goal-setting, check out *Ready Aim Fire! A Practical Guide to Setting and Achieving Goals* by Jim Woods and Erik Fisher.)

2. Write down your goals where you can see them often. A goal is not tangible until you write it down. I keep a list of my goals in the Evernote app. I have a separate note for each goal, where I include the specific goal (i.e. "lose 20 lbs. by June 30") as well as my motivations for achieving the goal (i.e. "Because I will feel better, look better, and have more energy for my work and family.")

I keep a list of all of my goals in an Evernote notebook called "Goals" (pretty creative title, eh?). I also have a shortcut to this notebook so I can access it quickly.

The tool isn't important. Use what works for you. The important thing is that you write down your goals and why you want to achieve them.

3. Track your progress and adjust as necessary. Every week, either on Sunday evening or Monday morning, I do a weekly review of my goals. I don't make progress every week. In fact, sometimes I fail miserably. That's okay because I know where I stand in relationship to the overall goal.

Each week I have a specific target for most of these

goals. (I don't work on every goal each week.) For instance, it might be losing 2 lbs., writing a certain number of words, or having a date night with my wife. I write this down in Evernote so it's a concrete target.

I also review my goals several times a week and make adjustments as necessary. I also establish targets one or two months in the future for specific projects such as a book launch or online course I need to finish.

4. Get support and accountability from friends. You will reach more of your goals if you share your progress with others. Being a part of a mastermind has been very important in helping me make progress toward my goals. Every week when we meet, I walk through the goals I set for the past week, how I did on each of them, and what I plan to do the coming week.

It's important to have a supportive team who will encourage you to be your best, but will also challenge you to reach higher than you would on your own.

5. Make a little progress every day. Darren Hardy, publisher of Success magazine, wrote a great book called *The Compound Effect*. The essence of the book is that successful people make positive incremental changes, and over time those changes produce huge results.

Success doesn't happen overnight. When you look at others who have been successful, remember that they have worked for years to get where they are. They have put in the time and are reaping the rewards of their effort.

Don't get discouraged when you see the distance between where you are and where you want to be. Success happens every day when you make good choices that propel you toward a better future.

Every single day counts. In fact, all you have are days. Your life is just a collection of years, and a year is just a collection of 365 days. Make every day count.

What's stopping you from doing something extraordinary over the next year? Could this be the best year of your life? It all begins with being intentional about setting goals and using your time.

When Michelangelo painted the Sistine Chapel, he began with a detailed plan. What's your plan? As an artist, you value creativity, fresh ideas and being spontaneous. But inspiration is worthless unless you follow it with action.

So dream your dreams, plan your plans, and take action. Over the course of a year you will be amazed at what you can accomplish when you set goals and make steady progress toward them.

Questions for Reflection

1. Do you have a goal-setting process? How has it worked for you so far?
2. Why is it important to write down your goals and track your progress?
3. Are you part of a mastermind, small group, or some other type of network where you can share your goals and receive encouragement? If

not, what are your plans to establish or participate in a group like this?
4. Think about the past year of your life. Were you intentional about setting goals, and did you meet them? How would your life be different today if you had worked on your goals every day for the last year?

Z is for Zither

Have you ever seen the 1949 movie *The Third Man*, starring Joseph Cotton and Orson Welles? If not, you definitely should. It's fantastic. (Apparently I like Orson Welles since I've referred to him several times in this book.)

The music for *The Third Man* is certainly unique. The movie's director, Carol Reed, was scouting locations for the film and happened upon the music of Anton Karas, a local zither player. He liked it so much he asked him to score the entire movie with zither music.[1]

It was quirky. Different. And totally awesome.

Audiences loved it as well. The main theme, called *The Harry Lime Theme* (after the main character), was a hit and went on to sell millions of copies.

There's a simple lesson here. Be yourself. Be unique. Be different. Be who you're created and called to be. Don't worry about the critics and naysayers. They are motivated by jealousy and the disappointment of their own failed dreams.

There are two reasons you should pursue your own path and be yourself instead of conforming to others' expectations:

1. When you're authentic, you honor God. God is the one who created you. The best way to honor his intentions for your life is to pursue art that gives you fulfillment and springs from your true gifts.

2. When you're authentic, you serve your audience well. You do your best work when you're passionate and engaged in your art. It's hard to be passionate when you're stuck in a role that doesn't fit you. You can't make great art trying to be a square peg in a round hole.

That's exactly what I felt like when I graduated from college. I attended a small Christian school in St. Louis and chose preaching as my major. I didn't feel a strong pull toward preaching, but I felt a call to vocational ministry. I grew up in a small rural church and we only had one pastor, so that's the only type of ministry I knew.

During my senior year of college, I preached at a tiny country church in southern Illinois. I loved the people but I struggled to feel excited about preaching. I was more excited about music and the arts, but there weren't many church staff openings available. (This was in the mid-90's, when full-time worship leaders weren't as common.)

I resigned myself to the fact that I would never be a great preacher, but I felt stuck.

Just before I graduated, one of our college professors visited a church that happened to be looking for a worship leader. My fiancé and I were excited to hear about it, and I interviewed at the church a few weeks later (after we were just married).

I got the job and spent eight fantastic years at the church. (And in a sign of God's great timing, my wife also interviewed for a position there and was accepted.)

If you've ever felt stuck in a rut...

If you've ever set your passion aside so you could do something more "practical"...

If you've ever resigned yourself to settling for less...

If you've ever felt like you didn't fit in...

If you've ever let others cast you in someone else's mold that doesn't fit you...

It's time to step out on faith, make a change, and become the artist you were created to be. It may take some time. You will pay a price. There will be moments when you feel like throwing in the towel. You will probably disappoint some people in the process. (And that's OK.)

But when you consider the alternative—living a mediocre life of regret and half-remembered dreams—how could you settle for anything less?

Don't let your life pass you by. Take responsibility for your destiny. Be unique. Be bold. Be different.

Somewhere in the world, a story is waiting that can only be scored with the music of your life and art. It's time to break out your zither.

Go ahead. The world is waiting.

Questions for Reflection

1. Do you feel called by God to be an artist? Have you ever struggled with that calling? (If so, that means you're normal!)
2. Have you ever felt pressured to accept a job or fill a role that didn't match your talents or interests? What did you learn from the experience?
3. Do you feel you are living an authentic life? If not, why not?
4. Has anyone ever criticized you for being different or pursuing your own path in life? As best as you can tell, what was their motive? Were they trying to help you or just being critical and negative?
5. Think about someone in your life who is pursuing a creative path. How can you encourage or help them be an authentic artist?

Epilogue: The Artist's Manifesto

We've covered a lot of ground in *The Artist's Suitcase*. We've journeyed together through twenty-six different chapters, each with lots of information. It's easy to overwhelmed by all the things you want to accomplish and the changes you want to make.

But being an artist is not just about finishing tasks or getting things done. It's far more about the direction you're headed.

As we come to end of our journey together, I invite you to read the following manifesto and join with me in becoming the artist God created you to be. I wrote it to remind myself that the future hasn't been created yet; I am the captain of my own destiny.

Ralph Waldo Emerson said, "Do not go where the path may lead. Go instead where there is no path and leave a trail."[1] Grab your suitcase—let's blaze some trails!

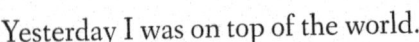

Yesterday I was on top of the world.

I was young and full of fire. I had my whole life ahead of me.

I stood on stage and basked in the attention. "You're great!" they said. "You have such a bright future ahead of you!" The sound of applause roared in my ears. I even won a contest or two.

They loved me! I was a success! I was somebody.

Yesterday I was going to conquer the world with my art. I was talented, gifted, amazing. At least, that's what everyone told me.

Then something happened.

Call it reality, call it discouragement, call it disappointment. Call it whatever you wish. If life is the school of hard knocks, I graduated Summa Cum Laude.

The flames of creative passion that once consumed me were little more than a wisp of smoke. My fresh ideas weren't so fresh anymore. The roar of the crowd became a deafening silence.

No more applause. No more medals or ribbons. No more approval.

I felt like a failure. A fraud. A ghost haunted by his own mediocrity.

How did things change so quickly? How did I go from being the young hotshot in the spotlight to the middle-aged guy watching from the sidelines?

Somewhere along the way I stopped dreaming about

the future and became content with recounting yesterday's triumphs. And the tales grew more stale with every telling.

My "Someday I'm going to . . ." turned into "When I was your age . . ."

Life became safe. Comfortable. Predictable. Boring.

Yesterday I was a success.

But yesterday didn't last forever.

Today I carry the weight of the world.

Mostly it's the weight of disappointment—disappointment at unfulfilled dreams, unmet expectations, and unreleased potential.

But it's not just that. To tell you the truth, I'm afraid.

Afraid? Really, at my age? Shouldn't I have moved past that by now? Not a chance.

So what am I afraid of?

I'm afraid that I won't be successful again. I'm afraid that I don't have what it takes. I'm afraid that yesterday's success was just dumb luck. I'm afraid that I'm worse than a has-been . . . I'm a never-once-was.

Most of all, I'm afraid that everyone will wake up and realize what I've known all along: I'm way in over my head and don't have a clue what I'm doing.

That leaves me with two choices: Stay where I am, paralyzed with fear . . . or move.

Even though I'm afraid—terrified, really—I must move. Every bone in my body screams, "Why risk it? You'll just be disappointed again! You're past your prime. Your best days are behind you. Just settle in and stay comfortable where it's safe."

But in the deepest recesses of my heart, I know the truth: comfort is never safe. In fact, comfort is the most dangerous place to live.

So today, I choose to move.

Today I will press on. Today I will rouse myself and give it my best shot. Not because I don't fear the future, but because I fear the present if it remains unchanged.

Today I choose to believe the best about myself while acknowledging my failures and learning from them.

Today I ignore the voice of fear telling me that I'm a failure, that I'll never amount to anything, that my best days are behind me, that no one cares about my work and my art.

Today I will take good care of my body, mind and soul because I can't give what I don't have. I'm not much use to anyone if I'm always sick, negative, and depressed.

Today I abandon my regrets and stop flogging myself for my mistakes. I release my grip on the baggage that has crushed my spirit for too long.

Today I push aside my doubts and face the future with faith—faith in myself, faith in my calling, and most important, faith in my God who has brought me this far.

Today I am secure in my purpose. I know who I am, and who I'm not. I accept my limitations—no, I embrace them. Because my limitations are just signposts pointing to new horizons.

Today I am thankful for all that has gone before, both

good and bad. Because yesterday's rain brings forth tomorrow's flowers.

Today there is fear, doubt, uncertainty.

But today won't last forever.

Tomorrow I will face the world.

I will face the world, not with the frown of a critic or the smirk of a cynic, but with the smile of a friend.

Because it's not just the world. It's my world.

It's my world because God put me here for a reason. I was born into this time, this place, to step into the unique purpose God has for me.

And if I don't do it, who will?

This is a long journey, and I'm unsure of what lies ahead. The question is not whether I will take the journey —everyone is taking a journey. The question is what kind of journey it will be.

Will it be joyful? Productive? Discouraging? Hopeful? Lonely? Full of worry and anxiety? Or full of hope and encouragement and community?

It's whatever I want it to be. It's all up to me.

So I'm ready to take this step forward with a new sense of purpose. I don't know my destination, but I know my direction. And for the first time in a long time, I feel hopeful and content.

Some say the journey of a thousand miles begins with a single step. I say it begins with just finding your shoes.

So tomorrow I will not only find them, I will tie my shoelaces and plant my feet on the edge of tomorrow. One step will become two, then ten, then hundreds, then thousands. And what is a successful journey except thousands of steps in the right direction?

Tomorrow I will head into the future knowing who I am and what I must do.

I'm an artist. An artist!

I will create with passion . . . because I can't *not* create.

I will lead by example . . . because my life speaks louder than my words.

I will reach for excellence . . . because a mediocre artist makes a mediocre difference.

I will join in community . . . because the journey is so much better with friends.

I will focus on the positive . . . because we don't need another jaded artist.

I will believe the best about others . . . because everyone is desperate for an encouraging word.

Yesterday my success gave way to failure.

Today my failure is giving birth to purpose.

And tomorrow my purpose helps give hope to the world.

Tomorrow there is joy. There is hope. There is encouragement. There is the kind of success that truly matters.

And tomorrow will last forever.

Questions for Reflection

1. At what point in your life have you most felt "on top of the world"? What was it about that time or those events that made it so significant?
2. Have you ever felt your creative passion drain away or experienced a period when your ideas seemed old and stale? What was that experience like? What do you think caused it?
3. How do you define "success" in your life? What does it mean for you to "win" or consider your work or your art a success? Do you feel successful right now? Why or why not?
4. What are the unfulfilled dreams in your life? Why haven't they become a reality?
5. Socrates said, "Know thyself." How well do you know yourself—your gifts, personality, passions, dreams, weaknesses, etc.? Do you have faith in yourself? Why or why not? Do you even like yourself?
6. Do you believe you were born for a reason? Do you believe you have a unique purpose? What is that purpose?

Quick Favor

Thanks so much for reading *The Artist's Suitcase*! I hope you enjoyed the book.

May I ask a quick favor? Will you take a moment to leave an honest review for *The Artist's Suitcase* on Amazon? Reviews are the BEST way to help others find and purchase the book.

You can visit the link below to share a quick review. I appreciate you!

KentSanders.net/SuitcaseReview

Gratitude

I used read books and wonder why the acknowledgements sections were so long. One person wrote the book, so why did they need to thank so many people? Now, having written two books, I understand why that's the case.

My wife Melanie has been my biggest fan and encourager since day one. She never wavered in her faith and encouragement. I love you!

Thanks to my son Ben, who keeps me going with his jokes, drawing, and our wrestling matches.

My Mom, Mary McEntire, has always believed in me and encouraged me to write. She is also a great book editor, and has combed every book for errors. My Dad, Don Sanders, and my older brother, also named Don Sanders, have also encouraged me as a writer.

My Junior High English teacher, Mrs. Mathis, was the first teacher to tell me I could be a writer. It would be hard to overestimate how great it feels to finally dedicate a book to her after almost 30 years. She is a testament to the fact that teachers can change lives.

Speaking of teachers, Kimanzi Constable, Dixie Gillaspie, and Jimmy Burgess have taught writing courses that have helped me become a better writer.

Jim Woods, Blake Atwood, and Chris Morris have given me lots of feedback and advice on writing. Jim also improved this book by providing first-rate editing!

Thanks so several key people who have been part of past or current masterminds and have given lots of feedback and accountability for my writing: Eric Elder, Justin Larson, Rye Taylor, Steve Spring, Ellory Wells, and Christy Piper. (Thanks to Eric for also writing the foreword and helping edit the book.)

Kristi Griffith is a gifted graphic designer, as evidenced by the fantastic job she did for the book cover.

I wrote the first draft of *The Artist's Suitcase* in Summer 2013, and it was required reading for my Introduction to the Arts class that Fall at St. Louis Christian College, where I teach. Thank you to all the students in that course for reading it, discussing it, and offering some helpful feedback.

Thanks to KC Proctor and ChurchMag Press for publishing my first book, *30 Days of Evernote for Churches*. It was a thoroughly positive experience and helped give me the confidence to move forward with *The Artist's Suitcase*.

I owe a special thank you to Dan Miller and all the members of 48 Days Eagles. It's a truly inspiring community of artists, entrepreneurs, writers, and movers and shakers. I literally couldn't have done this without the friendships and support I've received from the friends I've met there.

Thank you to the Artist's Suitcase Insiders Team, who helped launch this book and get the word out! It means the world that you believed in the message of this book enough to share it with others. You guys are the best!

The launch team included these friends: Melissa AuClair, Blake Atwood, Eric Elder, Liz Ellingwood, Pat Evrard, Darla Johnson (who gave helpful feedback), Ally Keaton, Henry Matlock (who also gave great feedback), Anna McConnaughhay, Aaron Murg, Christina Piper, Jason Pockrandt, Mark Revisky, Joshua Rivers, Rob Still, Jon Stolpe, and Elliot Voris.

Finally, I want to thank YOU for buying and reading this book. Your encouragement and support means a lot. Plus, you have helped me keep shoes on my son, who is growing so fast he needs a new pair every few months!

I know almost everyone says this, but my biggest thanks of all goes to God. He has put an amazing amount of people in my life who have helped me in too many ways to count. Thank you, God, for the opportunity to influence people through my words. I pray that I can help others as much as they have helped me.

Who is Kent Sanders?

Kent Sanders is the founder of Inkwell Ghostwriting, which helps leaders grow their business through books and other content. He is also the author of *The Artist's Suitcase: 26 Essentials for the Creative Journey* and co-author of *Performance-Driven Giving: The Roadmap to Unleashing the Power of Generosity in Your Life* with David Hancock and Bobby Kipper.

In addition to writing books for himself and his clients, Kent loves to help other writers. He is the host of the Daily Writer podcast, which helps writers cultivate the habits for creative success, and the founder of the Daily Writer membership community. He lives just outside of St. Louis and enjoys spending time outdoors with his wife and teenage son.

Email: Kent@KentSanders.net
Web: https://KentSanders.net
Twitter & Instagram: @KentSanders
Facebook: https://facebook.com/kentsanders
LinkedIn: https://linkedin.com/in/kent-sanders

The Daily Writer

Web: https://DailyWriterLife.com
Podcast: https://DailyWriterLife.com/Podcast
Instagram: @dailywriterlife
Community: https://DailyWriterLife.com/Community

Notes

A is for Attitude

1. John C. Maxwell, *The 21 Irrefutable Laws of Leadership*, 10th Anniversary Edition (Nashville: Thomas Nelson, 2007), 106.

B is for Blank Page

1. Steven Pressfield, *The War of Art* (New York: Grand Central Publishing, 2002), 16.

C is for Critics

1. Brad Bird, *Ratatouille*, directed by Brad Bird (Burbank, CA: Walt Disney Home Entertainment, 2005), DVD.
2. Theodore Roosevelt, "The Man in the Arena," (excerpt from the speech "Citizenship in a Republic" delivered at the Sorbonne, in Paris, France on April 23, 1910), accessed April 13, 2015, http://www.theodore-roosevelt.com/trsorbonnespeech.html.

D is for Doubt

1. Henry Ford quote, BrainyQuote, accessed May 13, 2015, http://www.brainyquote.com/quotes/quotes/h/henryford131621.html.

E is for Excellence

1. The Imagineers, *The Imagineering Way* (New York: Disney Enterprises, Inc., 2003), 48.

F is for Failure

1. C. S. Lewis quote, BrainyQuote, accessed April 23, 2015, http://www.brainyquote.com/quotes/quotes/c/cslewis119178.html

H is for Humility

1. For a video of the performance, watch "U2 / 'All I Want Is You' (w/ Adam Bevell) / Nashville / 2011-07-02 / 360 Tour" YouTube video, 4:16, posted by "PAPER DOLLING FILMS," July 4, 2011, https://www.youtube.com/watch?v=uURKYko6Q7c. Thanks to Jim Woods for bringing my attention to this story.
2. Saint Augustine quote, BrainyQuote, accessed April 23, 2015, http://www.brainyquote.com/quotes/quotes/s/saintaugus148548.html.

I is for Imperfections

1. What Goes On: The Beatles Anomalies List, accessed April 28, 2015, http://wgo.signal11.org.uk/wgo.htm.

J is for Just

1. Matthew J. Bruccoli, *F. Scott Fitzgerald: A Life in Letters* (New York: Scriber, 1995), 256.

K is for Key

1. Steven Spielberg quote, BrainyQuote, accessed April 23, 2015, http://www.brainyquote.com/quotes/quotes/s/stevenspie584069.html.
2. Philo quote, BrainyQuote, accessed April 23, 2015, http://www.brainyquote.com/quotes/quotes/p/philo103409.html.

L is for Love

1. Herman J. Mankiewicz and Orson Welles, *Citizen Kane*, directed by Orson Welles (1941; Burbank, CA: Warner Bros., 2011), DVD.
2. Henri Nouwen, *In the Name of Jesus: Reflections on Christian Leadership* (New York: The Crossroad Publishing Company, 1992), 43-44.

M is for Mind

1. James Allen, *As a Man Thinketh*, accessed April 2, 2015, http://jamesallen.wwwhubs.com/think.htm.
2. Earl Nightingale, *The Strangest Secret*, accessed March 14, 2015, http://www.nightingale.com/articles/the-strangest-secret/.

N is for Napkin

1. John Wooden, *Wooden: A Lifetime of Observations and Reflections On and Off the Court* (Chicago: Contemporary Books, 1997), 84-85.
2. "Fanny Crosby," Christianity Today, accessed April 24, 2015, http://www.christianitytoday.com/ch/131christians/poets/crosby.html.

O is for Old Things

1. Saint Athanasius, *On the Incarnation* (Yonkers, NY: St. Vladimir's Seminary Press, 2012), 3.
2. Walter Isaaacson, *Steve Jobs* (New York: Simon & Schuster, 2011), 25-26, 207-208, 415-416.

P is for Persistence

1. Ralph Waldo Emerson quote, BrainyQuote, accessed May 2, 2015, http://www.brainyquote.com/quotes/quotes/r/ralphwaldo386697.html.

2. Gillian Zoe Segal, *Getting There: A Book of Mentors* (New York: Abram Image, 2015), 26.

S is for Secure

1. "Insecure," *The American Heritage® Stedman's Medical Dictionary*, Houghton Mifflin Company, accessed May 15, 2015, http://dictionary.reference.com/browse/insecure.
2. Disney Book Group, *The Quotable Walt Disney* (New York: Disney Enterprises, Inc., 2001), 247.

T is for Time

1. "Average Commute Times," WNYC, accessed March 24, 2015, http://project.wnyc.org/commute-times-us/embed.html#5.00/42.000/-89.500.

X is for Xerox

1. Oscar Wilde quote, GoodReads, accessed May 16, 2015, http://www.goodreads.com/quotes/19884-be-yourself-everyone-else-is-already-taken.

Z is for Zither

1. A zither is a stringed instrument that's sort of a cross between a guitar and a dulcimer. It's played around the world but most commonly in Eastern Europe. If you've seen episodes of SpongeBob Squarepants, the Hawaiian-themed music during the end credits sounds a little like zither music.

Epilogue: The Artist's Manifesto

1. Ralph Waldo Emerson quote, BrainyQuote, accessed May 17, 2015, http://www.brainyquote.com/quotes/quotes/r/ralphwaldo101322.html.

Made in USA - North Chelmsford, MA
1105955_9781515011880
03.22.2022 1656